P9-DTW-781

AENEAS

B. A. Hoena

Consultant:
Dr. Laurel Bowman
Department of Greek and Roman Studies
University of Victoria
Victoria, British Columbia

Capstone
press
Mankato, Minnesota

DISCARD
CARLSBAD CITY LIBRARY
1775 Dove Ln.
Carlsbad, CA 92011

ALCO
LIT
292.13
HOE

Capstone Press
151 Good Counsel Drive, P.O. Box 669, Mankato, Minnesota 56002
www.capstonepress.com

Copyright © 2004 by Capstone Press. All rights reserved.
No part of this publication may be reproduced in whole or in part, or stored in a retrieval
system, or transmitted in any form or by any means, electronic, mechanical, photocopying,
recording, or otherwise, without written permission of the publisher.
For information regarding permission, write to Capstone Press,
151 Good Counsel Drive, P.O. Box 669, Dept. R, Mankato, Minnesota 56002.
Printed in the United States of America

Library of Congress Cataloging-in-Publication Data
Hoena, B. A.
    Aeneas / by B. A. Hoena.
    p. cm. — (World mythology)
    Summary: An introduction to the character of Aeneas and his importance in Greek and
Roman mythology.
    Includes bibliographical references and index.
    ISBN 0-7368-2496-0 (hardcover)
    1. Aeneas (Legendary character)—Juvenile literature. 2. Mythology, Roman—Juvenile
literature. [1. Aeneas (Legendary character) 2. Mythology, Classical.] I. Title. II. Series:
World mythology (Mankato, Minn.)
BL820.A34H64 2004
398.2'0937'02—dc22   2003012973

Editorial Credits

Juliette Peters, series designer; Patrick Dentinger, book designer and illustrator;
    Alta Schaffer, photo researcher; Eric Kudalis, product planning editor

Photo Credits

Art Resource/Erich Lessing, 6, 10; Réunion des Musées Nationaux, 12; Scala, 14, 16, 20
Bridgeman Art Library/Louvre, Paris, France/Peter Willi, 8; Private Collection, 4
Capstone Press/Gary Sundermeyer/Ilias Papadopoulos, cover (helmet), 1, 18
Corbis/Araldo de Luca, cover (statue)

2 3 4 5 6 09 08 07 06 05

MAR 1 0 2008

TABLE OF CONTENTS

The Burning of Troy by Nicolas Poussin shows Aeneas (center) fleeing from the burning city of Troy. Aeneas is carrying his injured father, Anchises.

AENEAS

Prince Aeneas (ih-NEE-uhss) was a great Trojan hero. During the Trojan War, he fought to defend the city of Troy from a Greek army. Aeneas was wounded by the Greek hero Diomedes (dye-uh-MEE-deez) in one battle. Luckily, Aeneas' mother, Venus, was a goddess. She saved him from being killed.

After ten years of fighting, neither the Greeks nor the Trojans could win the war. Then one night, Aeneas woke to the sounds of clashing swords. The Greeks had found a way inside the city. Aeneas knew he had to escape or he would be killed. He fled as the Greeks burned Troy to the ground.

After his escape, Aeneas asked the god Apollo what he should do. Apollo told Aeneas to lead the Trojans to a faraway land called Italy. There, Aeneas would start a great new kingdom. Aeneas had many adventures on his way to Italy.

Virgil sits between two Muses in this ancient Roman mosaic. In myths, Muses were goddesses who inspired people to create art and poetry.

Stories about heroes like Aeneas are called **quest** myths. In these stories, heroes performed very difficult tasks. Quest myths encouraged people. They taught people never to give up even if a task seemed impossible.

The Greek poet Homer lived around 800 B.C. He is famous for his quest myths *The Iliad* and *The Odyssey*. *The Iliad* tells about the last year of the Trojan War. *The Odyssey* tells about the Greek hero Odysseus (oh-DISS-ee-uhss) and his journey home after the war.

Another famous quest myth was written by Virgil. Virgil was a Roman poet born about 70 B.C. His poem *The Aeneid* tells of Aeneas' adventures after the Trojan War.

Virgil died before he finished writing *The Aeneid*. In his **will**, Virgil asked that *The Aeneid* be burned. The Roman Emperor Augustus did not allow Virgil's work to be destroyed. Augustus wanted to keep *The Aeneid*. It told the myth of how the Roman Empire began.

Aeneas (center) meets his mother, Venus, in Pietro da Cortona's painting *Venus Appearing to Aeneas as a Huntress*.

AENEAS' BIRTH

Venus was the goddess of love. She liked playing tricks on the male gods. She made them fall in love with mortal women. Gods were embarrassed to be in love with humans.

Jupiter was ruler of the gods. He wanted to teach Venus a lesson and embarrass her. Jupiter made Venus fall in love with a mortal man, Prince Anchises (an-KEYE-seez). Anchises lived near Troy. Venus and Anchises were Aeneas' parents.

Venus did not want anyone to know she was Aeneas' mother. Anchises said he would not tell, but he broke his promise. As ruler of the gods, Jupiter punished people who broke their promises. Jupiter struck Anchises with a lightning bolt, injuring Anchises' legs. For the rest of his life, Anchises had difficulty walking.

After Aeneas' birth, Venus left her son with some nymphs. The nymphs raised Aeneas until he was 5. Then, he went to live with his father. Venus did not help raise Aeneas, but she watched over him. She kept him safe during his adventures.

This ancient clay pot was made about 700 B.C. It shows soldiers hiding in the hollow horse made by the Greek army. The horse is known as the Trojan horse.

THE TROJAN WAR

Myths say that Helen was the most beautiful woman in the world. Prince Paris of Troy took Helen from her husband, Greek Prince Menelaus (men-uh-LAY-uhss). The Trojan War began when Menelaus led a Greek army to the city of Troy to get Helen back.

In myths, the walls around Troy were built by gods. The walls were too tall for the Greeks to climb over and too strong to knock down. But the Greek hero Odysseus had an idea. He had a huge, hollow horse built of wood. One night, Odysseus left the horse in front of the city gates. Then, the Greek army hid from the Trojans.

In the morning, the Trojans thought the Greek army had left. They also believed the huge wooden horse was a gift from the gods. The Trojans rolled the horse inside the city. They did not know that some Greek soldiers were hiding inside the horse.

That night, the Greek soldiers climbed out of the horse. They opened the city gates. The Greek army then came out of hiding. The Greek army entered Troy and defeated the Trojans.

Harpies attack Aeneas (standing left) and the Trojans in François Perrier's painting *Aeneas and His Companions Fighting the Harpies.*

FLIGHT FROM TROY

After the Trojan War, Aeneas gathered up as many Trojans and ships as he could find. He sailed away from Troy. He hoped to escape the Greek army and find a new place to live.

First, Aeneas sailed to the island of Delos (DEH-lohss). He visited Apollo's oracle on the island. In myths, gods spoke to people through oracles. Apollo spoke through his oracle and told Aeneas to sail west to Italy. There, Aeneas would start a great new kingdom that would rule the world.

On their journey west, the Trojans stopped on the islands of Strophades (STROH-fay-deez). They went ashore to get food and were attacked by Harpies. These monsters had the lower bodies of birds and the upper bodies of women. The Harpies stunk like garbage, screeched loudly, and attacked with sharp claws.

Next, the Trojans sailed to Sicily. One-eyed giants called Cyclopes (sye-KLOH-peez) lived on this island. The Cyclopes were very strong and stood as tall as trees.

Aeneas (bottom center, right) looks for his father in Jan the Elder Brueghel's painting *Sibyl Leading Aeneas to the Underworld*.

During his journey, Aeneas sailed to the city of Carthage in northern Africa. He fell in love with the city's queen, Dido. But Jupiter did not allow them to stay together. Jupiter told Aeneas that he had to leave Dido and sail to Italy. Aeneas knew Jupiter would punish him if he did not obey. As Aeneas sailed away, Dido died because she was sad that he was leaving.

Aeneas' father had died earlier in the journey to Italy. After leaving Carthage, Aeneas saw Anchises' ghost. The ghost told Aeneas that Anchises had something to tell him. Aeneas went to the Underworld to hear what his father had to say. In myths, people went to the Underworld after they died.

Anchises warned his son about a great war that Aeneas would have to fight in Italy. He also encouraged his son. Anchises told Aeneas that his kingdom in Italy would be very powerful. Anchises told Aeneas about great men like Augustus and Julius Caesar. These men would become rulers of Aeneas' kingdom.

The Death of Turnus was painted by Niccolò dell' Abate. It shows Aeneas defeating Turnus in battle.

AENEAS IN ITALY

After leaving the Underworld, Aeneas sailed to Italy. He came to the kingdom of King Latinus (luh-TYE-nuhss) and Queen Amata (ah-MUH-tuh).

Latinus did not have a male **heir** to become king after he died. Latinus had a daughter named Lavinia (luh-VIN-ee-uh). Many men in Italy wanted to marry her and become king. But years ago, Latinus was told that his daughter would marry a stranger from another land. When Aeneas landed in Italy, the king knew his daughter was meant to marry Aeneas.

Queen Amata did not want Lavinia to marry Aeneas. She wanted her to marry an Italian man named Turnus (TUR-nuhss). Amata told Turnus to go to war with Aeneas and the Trojans.

Venus helped Aeneas in battle. She had her husband, Vulcan, make Aeneas a sword and a shield. Aeneas then challenged Turnus to a fight. With his new weapons, Aeneas defeated Turnus. He married Lavinia and became king of Italy.

GREEK and ROMAN *Mythical Figures*

Greek Name: **ANCHISES**
Roman Name: **ANCHISES**
Aeneas' father

Greek Name: **APHRODITE**
Roman Name: **VENUS**
Aeneas' mother and goddess of love and beauty

Greek Name: **APOLLO**
Roman Name: **APOLLO**
God of light, youth, and music

Greek Name: **DIDO**
Roman Name: **DIDO**
Queen of Carthage

Greek Name: **HELEN**
Roman Name: **HELEN**
Menelaus' wife

Greek Name: **HEPHAESTUS**
Roman Name: **VULCAN**
Venus' husband and god of fire

Greek Name: **MENELAUS**
Roman Name: **MENELAUS**
Greek prince married to Helen

Greek Name: **ODYSSEUS**
Roman Name: **ULYSSES**
Greek hero

Greek Name: **PARIS**
Roman Name: **PARIS**
Trojan prince who took Helen from Menelaus

Greek Name: **ZEUS**
Roman Name: **JUPITER**
Ruler of the sky and the gods

ROMAN AND GREEK MYTHS

Ancient Romans used myths of Aeneas to explain the beginnings of their people. They believed Aeneas and the Trojans founded the Roman Empire. The Roman Empire conquered much of the known world. About 100 B.C., the Romans took over Greece.

The Romans often used parts of cultures from countries they captured. Many Roman myths are copied from Greek stories. Virgil's *The Aeneid* is similar to Homer's *The Odyssey*. Both stories tell about a hero's adventures after the Trojan War. Aeneas and Odysseus also have similar adventures. They both meet the Cyclopes and go to the Underworld.

The Romans often changed the names of gods and characters from Greek myths. Venus is the Roman name for the Greek goddess of love, Aphrodite (a-fruh-DYE-tee). Jupiter is the Roman name for the Greek god Zeus (ZOOSS). Odysseus was known as Ulysses (yoo-LI-seez) in Roman myths.

Dido and Aeneas was painted by Jacopo Amigoni. The story of Dido and Aeneas is a popular love story in myths and art.

MYTHOLOGY TODAY

Long ago, storytellers traveled from village to village telling myths to people. Myths about heroes encouraged people. Other myths explained why things happened. For example, myths about Venus explained why people fell in love.

Today, myths inspire people. The stories of Aeneas and Odysseus were early adventure stories. Many stories are based on the adventures these heroes had. Henry Purcell wrote the opera *Dido and Aeneas* about the love story of Dido and Aeneas. Irish author James Joyce based his book *Ulysses* on the adventures of Odysseus.

People no longer believe that Greek and Roman myths are true. Today, myths are told for people's enjoyment and to help them learn. Myths are exciting stories. They also help people understand ancient cultures. People read myths to learn what people believed long ago.

Tiber River

• Rome

ITALY

Adriatic Sea

N
W • E
S

GREECE

• Troy

Aegean Sea

ITHACA

• Thebes

Ionian Sea

• Athens

• DELOS

STROPHADES

Sparta •

SICILY

Carthage •

TUNISIA

CRETE

Mediterranean Sea

SCALE
Miles
0   100   200

0   100   200
Kilometers

KEY
• City
⛰ Mount Olympus

22

GLOSSARY

ancient (AYN-shunt)—very old

culture (KUHL-chur)—a people's way of life, ideas, art, customs, and traditions

Cyclopes (sye-KLOH-peez)—giants with one eye in the middle of their foreheads

heir (AIR)—a person who has been left money or a title

mortal (MOR-tuhl)—not able to live forever; humans are mortal.

nymph (NIMF)—a female spirit or goddess found in a meadow, a forest, a mountain, or a stream

oracle (OR-uh-kuhl)—a place or thing that a god speaks through

quest (KWEST)—a journey taken by a hero to perform a task

Trojan (TROH-juhn)—a person from the ancient city of Troy, or having to do with the city of Troy, such as the Trojan War

Underworld (UHN-dur-wurld)—the place under the earth where spirits of the dead go

will (WIL)—written instructions stating what should happen to a person's belongings when that person dies

READ MORE

Hoena, B. A. *Venus.* World Mythology. Mankato, Minn.: Capstone Press, 2003.

Innes, Brian. *Myths of Ancient Rome.* Mythic World. Austin, Texas: Raintree Steck-Vaughn, 2001.

USEFUL ADDRESSES

**National Junior Classical
    League**
422 Wells Mill Drive
Miami University
Oxford, OH 45056

Ontario Classical Association
P.O. Box 19505
55 Bloor Street West
Toronto, ON M4W 1A5
Canada

INTERNET SITES

FactHound offers a safe, fun way to find Internet sites related to this book.
All of the sites on FactHound have been researched by our staff.

Here's how:
1. Visit *www.facthound.com*
2. Type in this special code **0736824960** for age-appropriate
   sites. Or enter a search word related to this book for a
   more general search.
3. Click on the **Fetch It** button.

FactHound will fetch the best sites for you!

INDEX